Christian Nursery Rhymes

Adapted by
Beverly Rae Charette

Illustrated by
Janet & Anne Graham Johnstone

Ideals Publishing Corp.
Milwaukee, Wisconsin

Copyright © MCMLXXXII by Dean & Son, Ltd.
All rights reserved. Printed and bound in U.S.A.
Published simultaneously in Canada.
ISBN 0-8249-8038-7

Pease porridge hot,
Pease porridge cold,
Pease porridge in the pot,
Nine days old.

I like it hot;
Brother likes it cold,
But we'll all thank God and share it
When it's nine days old.

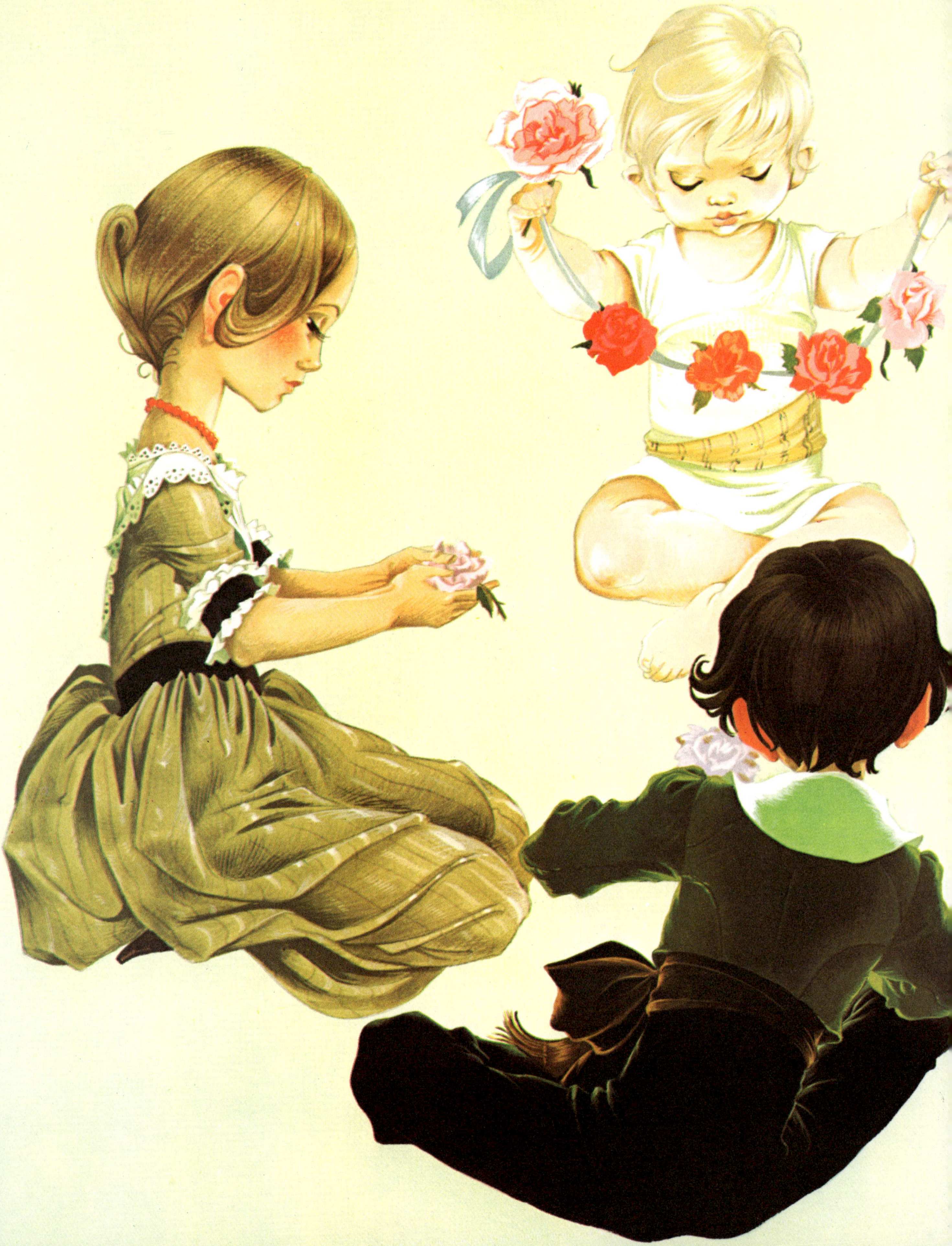

Ring-around-a-rosy,
God made all the posies;
One, two, three,
And God made me!

Rain, rain,
Always there
When it's needed,
Through God's care.

Rain, rain,
Sign of love,
Gift of life
From God above.

April showers,
March winds blow,
Glad that God
Makes it so.

Sir, in this garden that you groom,
Do you think there will be room
For all the plants to sprout and bloom?

Little friend, I have no doubt
All good things have room to sprout,
Our dear Lord will help them out.

If God's the One who sends each shower
To make the plants grow tall and flower,
Can He help me with His great power?

Why, look at me! Until I grew
I used to be as small as you.
Trust in Him; He'll help you, too.

But why must growing take so long?
And when will I be tall and strong?
Maybe I am growing wrong.

Come now, fellow, don't be glum;
Someday you'll be bigger, son,
Thanks to help from God's green thumb!

Gregory Griggs, Gregory Griggs
Had twenty-seven different wigs.
He wore them up; he wore them down
To please the people of the town.
He wore them east; he wore them west;
But the one God gave him he loved the best.

Mrs. Mason bought a basin.
Mrs. Tyson said, "What a nice one."
"What did it cost?" said Mrs. Frost;
"Half a crown," said Mrs. Brown.
"Did it indeed?" said Mrs. Reed;
"It did for certain," said Mrs. Burton.
　　　　　　Then Mrs. Nix, up to her tricks,
　　　　　　Dropped the basin on the bricks;
　　　　　　But Mrs. Mason then forgave her
　　　　　　As we are taught by our dear Savior.

If I would dig for treasure
So great I could not measure
The wealth it held for me,

I would not dig for gold;
I'd dig inside my soul
And find God's love for me.

Once I saw a little bird
Come hop, hop, hop;
So I cried, "Little bird,
Will you stop, stop, stop?"
Then I went to the window to say,
"How do you do?"
And he shook his little tail and said,
"How do you do, too?"

I asked my friend to sing me
Something sweet, sweet, sweet,
So he puffed up his chest
And sang, "Tweet, tweet, tweet,
I have come to spread the Gospel
And to ask you if you will
Spread it also." And I nodded
From across the windowsill.

When he had finished telling me
His message, off he flew;
Now I can pass the Good News on,
Especially to you: Jesus lives!

What are little boys made of, made of?
What are little boys made of?
Frogs and snails and puppy-dogs' tails,
And that's what little boys are made of.

What are little girls made of, made of?
What are little girls made of?
Sugar and spice and all that's nice,
And that's what little girls are made of.

What are all children
   made of, made of?
What are all children made of?
Love from the Father
   from whom all things come
And that's what all children
   are made of.

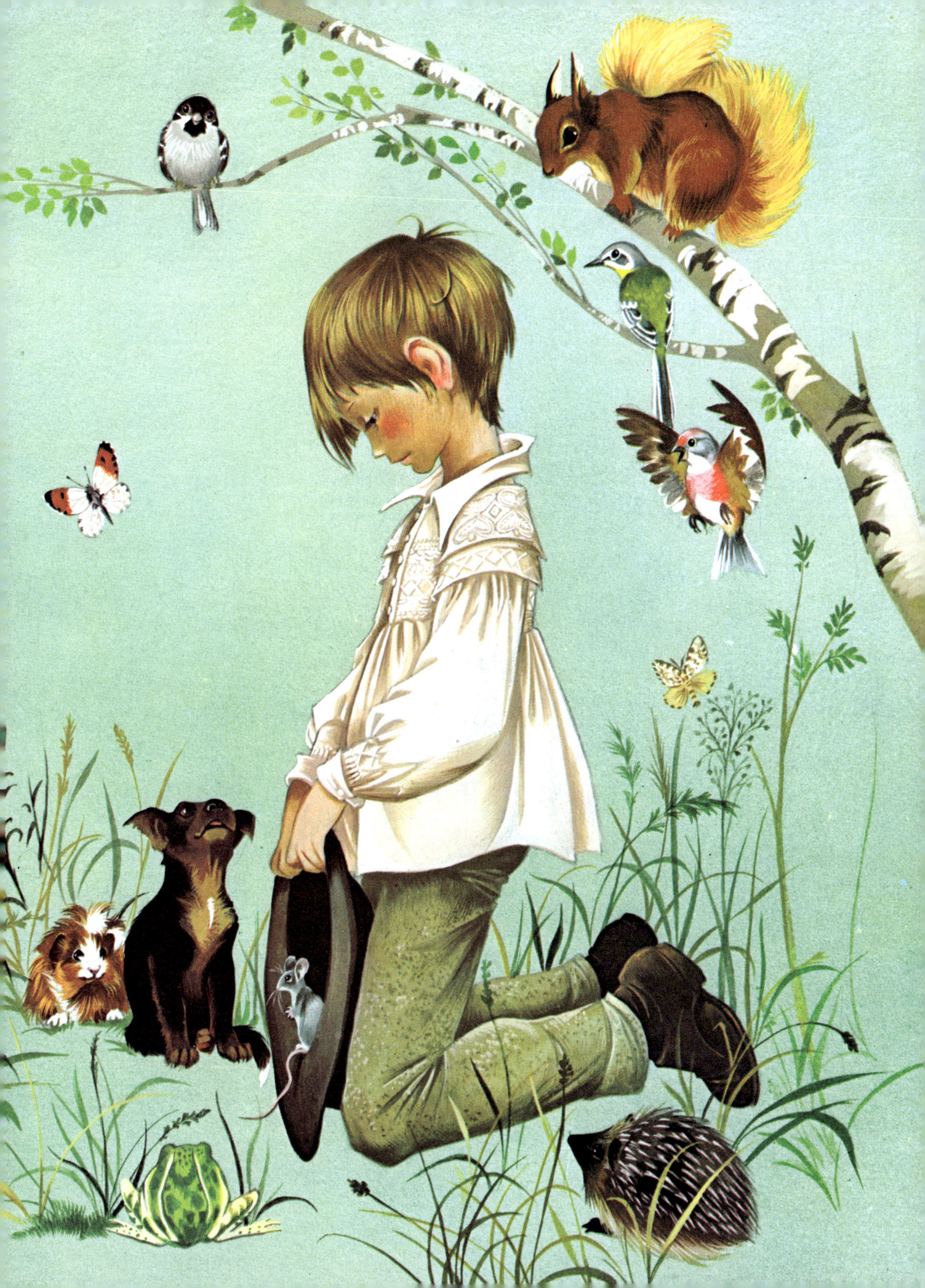

To Jordan, to Jordan,
To wash away sins;
Home again, home again,
My soul the Lord wins!

    To Jordan, to Jordan,
    To hear the dear Lord;
    Home again, home again,
    To spread His Word!

        In Heaven, in Heaven
        We'll all someday be
        And live with the Lord
        Through eternity!

Here we go round the mulberry bush,
The mulberry bush, the mulberry bush;
Here we go round the mulberry bush
On a frosty Christmas morning.

This is the way we greet the Lord,
Greet the Lord, greet the Lord;
This is the way we greet the Lord
On a frosty Christmas morning.

This is the way we sing "Amen,"
Sing "Amen," sing "Amen";
This is the way we sing "Amen"
On a frosty Christmas morning.

Little Betty Blue
Lost her holiday shoe;
What can little Betty do?
Her shoe, she'll have to get,
Although it will be wet.
God helps those who help themselves;
This truth she can't forget.

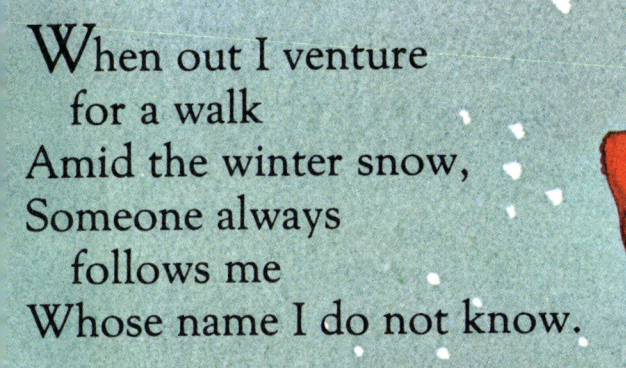

When out I venture
   for a walk
Amid the winter snow,
Someone always
   follows me
Whose name I do not know.

He won't come
   when it's sunny,
Just when there's snow or rain;
I turn around—
   he isn't there,
But he was there just the same.

But Someone else
   is *always* with me;
Of that I never fear;
For Jesus Christ
   has promised us
He'd be forever near.

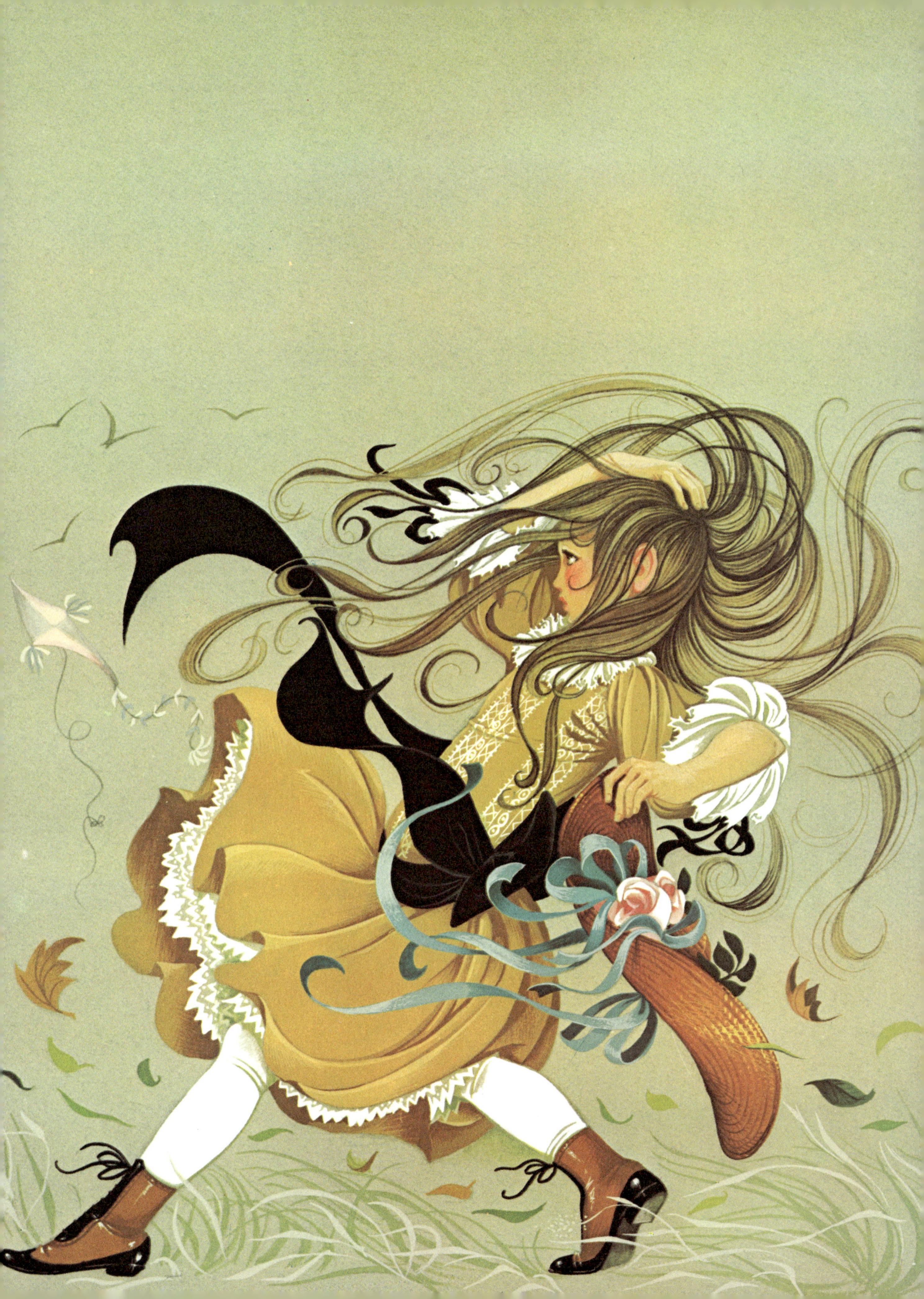

As I was going along,
   long, long,
A-singing a favorite song,
   song, song,
The wind blew suddenly strong,
   strong, strong
Till I thought something was wrong,
   wrong, wrong.

But I said to myself, "Oh, dear,
   dear, dear,
I need not ever fear,
   fear, fear;
That powerful wind I hear,
   hear, hear
Is just God saying He's near,
   near, near."

A fisher of fish,
I'm good at this
As you can plainly see.
A fisher of men,
The Lord said He
Would make me certainly.

"But what is the bait
For a fish so great?"
I asked Him curiously.
He said, "My love
For everyone
Is all the bait you need."

Blow, wind, blow; and go, mill, go;
That the miller may grind his corn;
That the baker may take it
And into bread make it
And send us some on Easter morn.

Blow, wind, blow; and go, mill go;
For Christ rose from death on this day.
In order to save us,
The Bread of Life He gave us;
Let's rejoice and share it today!

Rum-tat-a-tum!
Rum-tat-a-tum!
Johnny, beat the drum.

Rum-tat-a-tum!
Rum-tat-a-tum!
Marching, here we come.

We are Christian soldiers
Marching for the Lord,
Fitted out for combat,
Armed with the Word!

No one can defeat us
In spreading the Good News!
With "God Is Love" as battle cry,
How could we lose?

Rum-tat-a-tum!
Rum-tat-a-tum!
God gave His only Son!

Rum-tat-a-tum!
Rum-tat-a-tum!
God is number one!

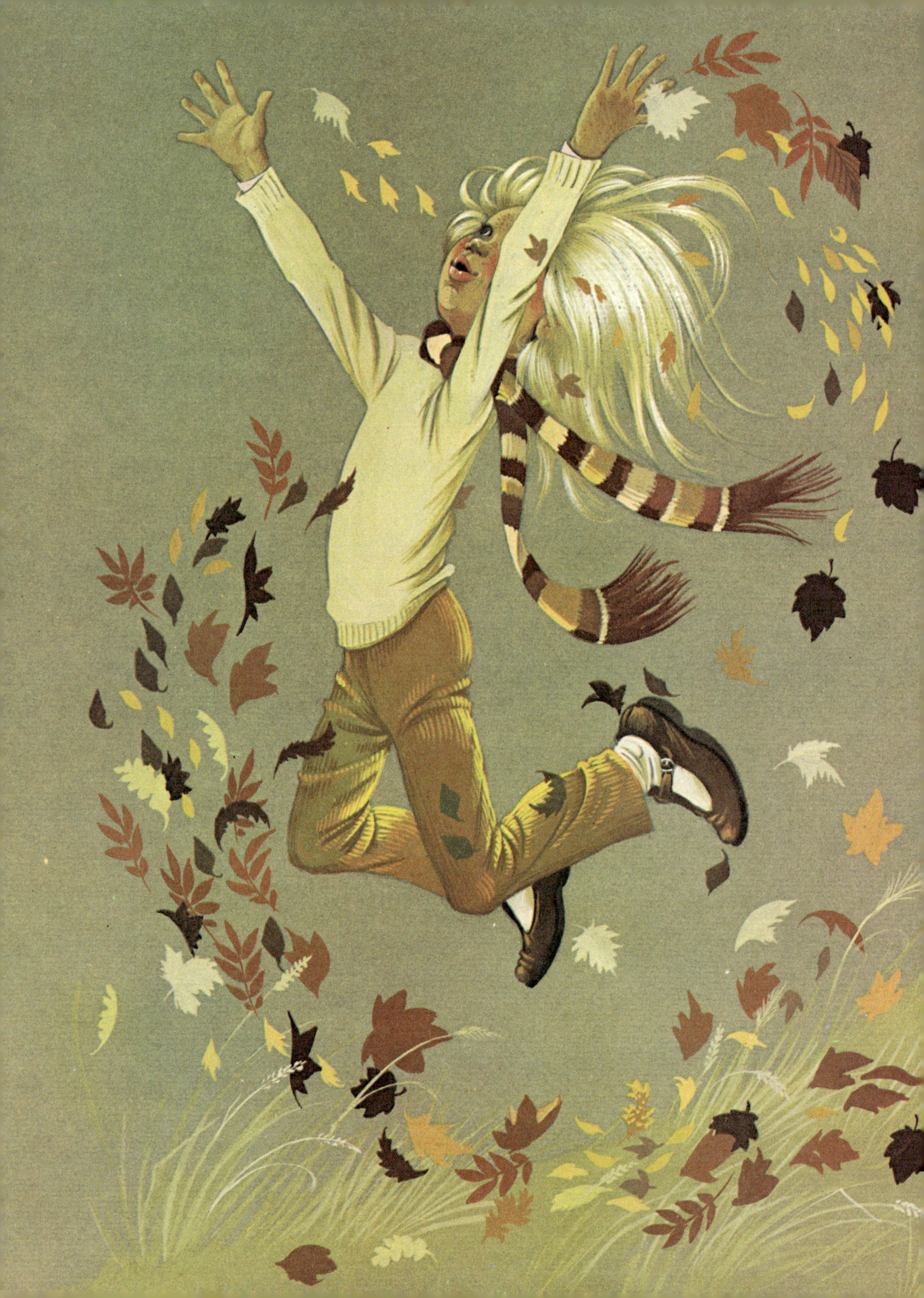

Jack and Jill
Went down the hill
On their way from Sunday School;
They rejoiced on the way
Because on this day
They had learned the Golden Rule.

"Do unto others,
Both sisters and brothers,
As you would have them do to you";
Each lovely word
Has come from the Lord,
And each is most certainly true.

I love my little donkey gray,
His shoulders crossed with black
To show that Jesus, so they say,
Once rode a donkey's back.
Oh, Jesus, teach us too, I pray,
To care for little donkeys gray.

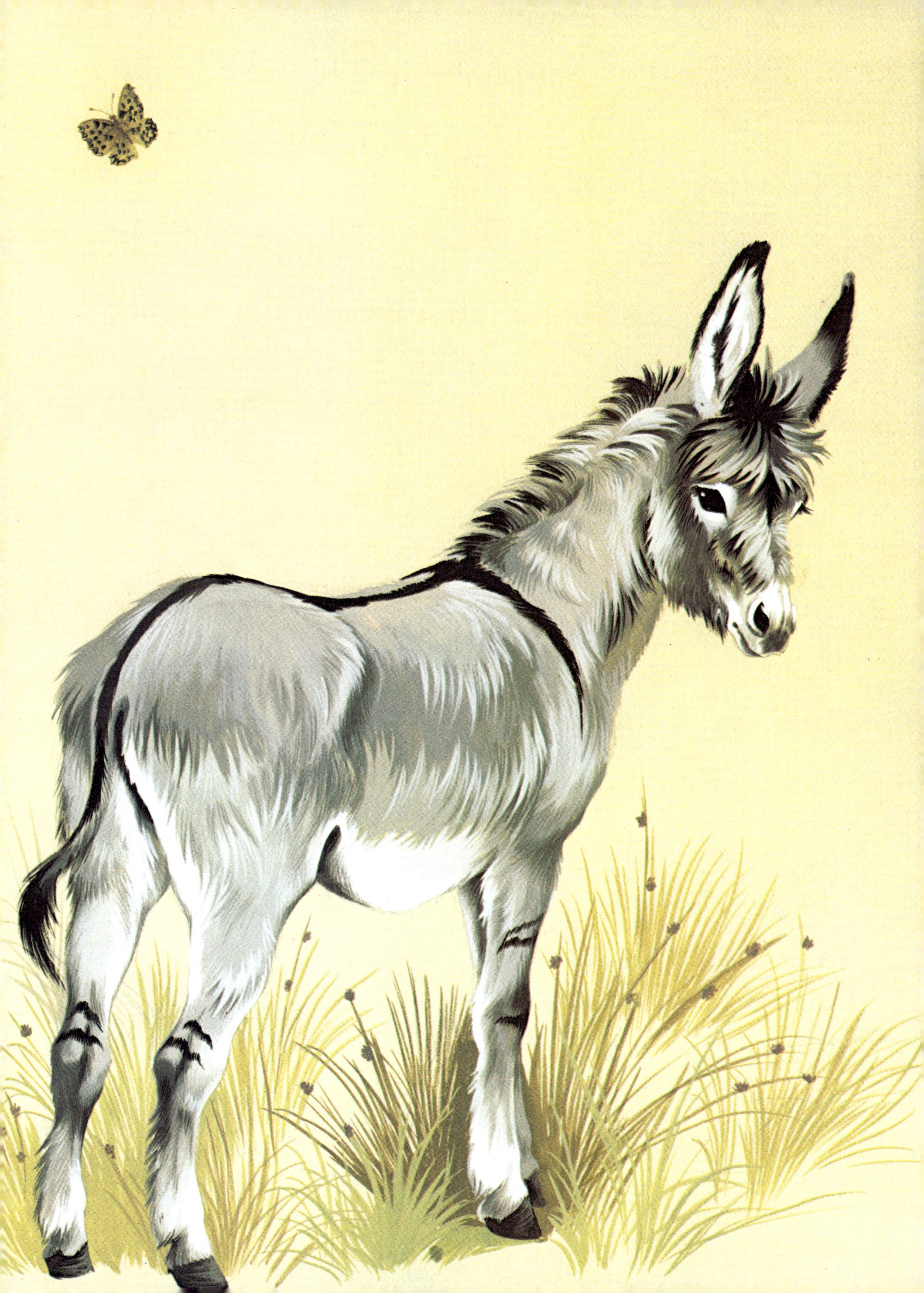

I had a little pony;
His name was
  Dapple Gray;
I lent him to a lady
To ride a mile away.

She whipped him, she slashed him,
She rode him through the mire;
I would not lend my pony now
For all the lady's hire.

A pony must be treated
With kindness and with care;
For he's one of God's creatures
With whom this world we share.

Ride a cock-horse to Banbury Cross
To see a fine lady upon a white horse;
With rings on her fingers and bells on her toes,
She'll praise the Lord with music wherever she goes.

Cushy cow, bonny,
Please grant my request;
I have need of your milk
For a small, hungry guest;
A small, hungry guest,
So tender and pure,
He's the true Son of God,
Of that I'm quite sure.

The loss of your milk,
Gentle cow, do not grieve,
For remember 'tis better
To give than receive;
To give, not receive,
Yes, that is the key,
For that's what God's Son does
For you and for me.

When I was at play,
I looked far away
To see if God's Kingdom I'd find.

But search as I might,
It was nowhere in sight;
His Kingdom just isn't that kind.

It isn't up high,
Away in the sky;
I should have known that
    from the start.

It's really quite near;
In fact, it's right here—
God's Kingdom is here
    in my heart!

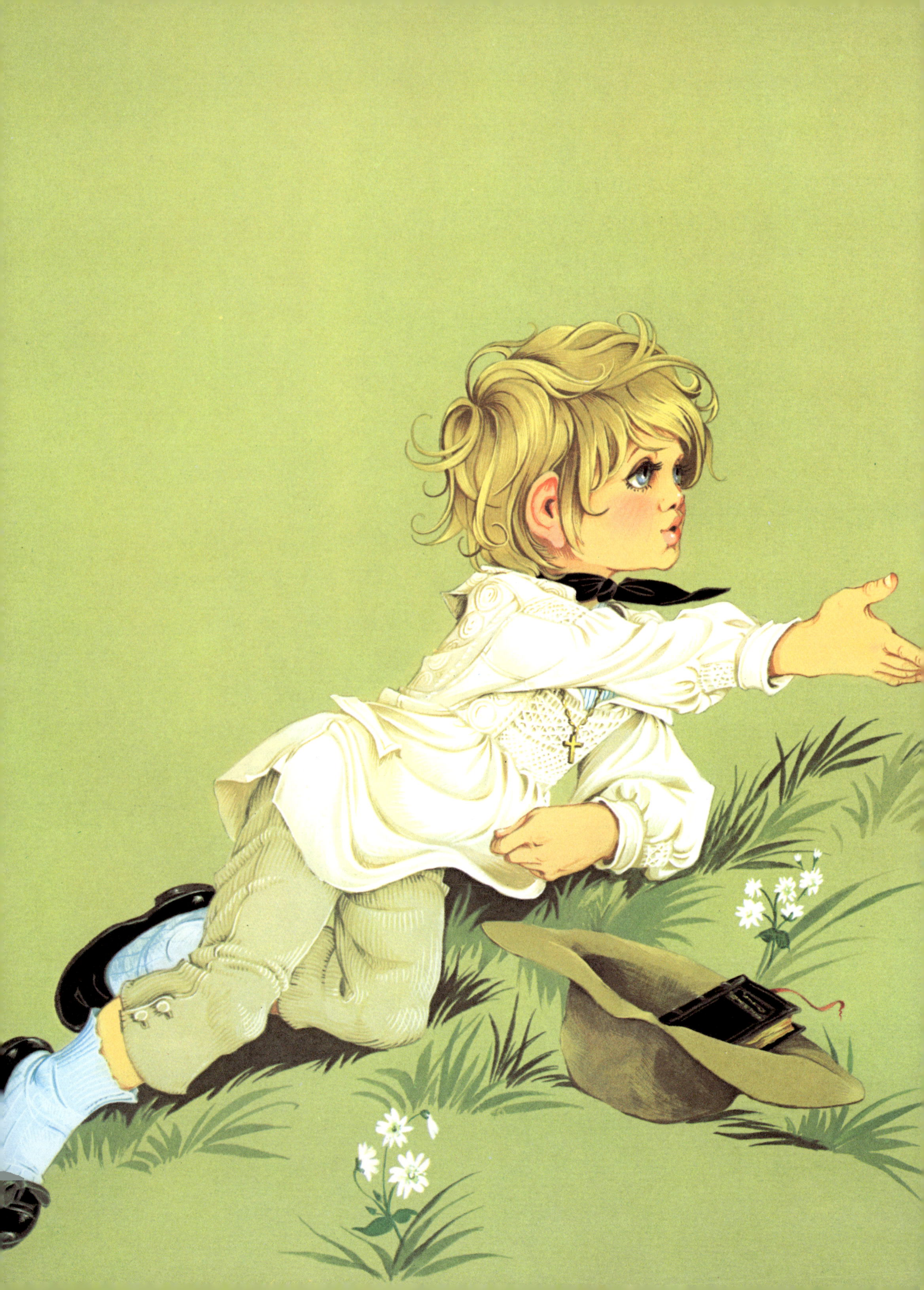

Baa, baa, little lamb,
Have you any wool?
Yes, sir, yes, sir,
Three bags full.

One for God the Father,
One for Christ, His Son,
And one for the Holy Ghost—
All three are God in one!

Grandmother O'Leary
Always is so cheery;
Days when it seems dreary she is glad.

When it's fiercely snowing,
Icy winds are blowing,
Gram says it's not going to be so bad.

If I say it's cold,
Gram will gently scold,
"Emphasize the good
Just as Jesus would."

Gram sets me to thinking;
All bad thoughts are shrinking;
They're gone in the winking of an eye.

Isn't it a wonder
We don't always ponder
On the good things under God's blue sky?

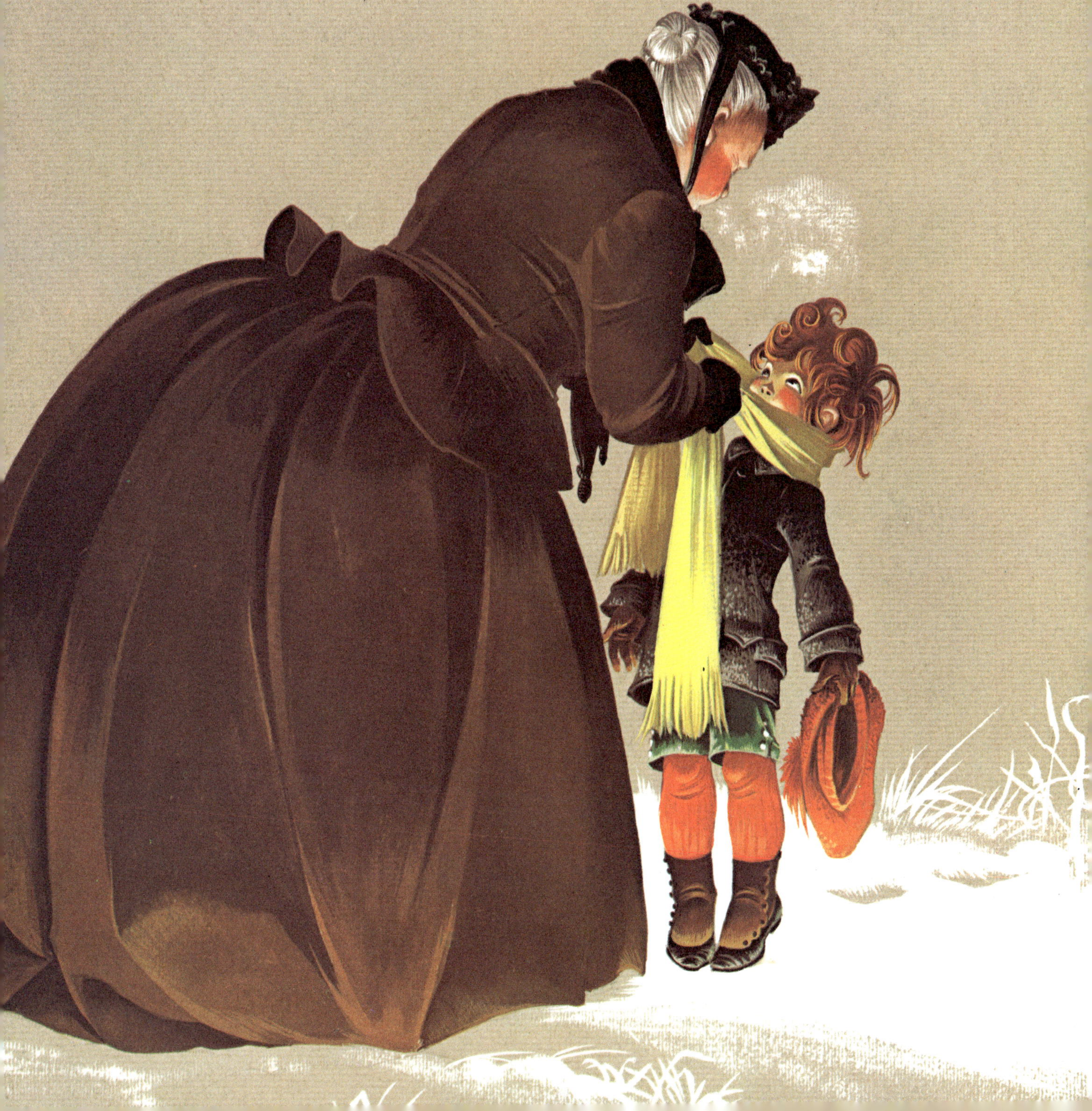

Lully-lu-lye, lully-lu-lye,
Sing my baby a soft lullaby.

Lully-lu-lye, lully-lu-lye,
To dreamland she sails off through the sky.

And who pulls the cradle?
Six horses are able
To follow the straight, narrow road.

And Babe follows after
With sweet, happy laughter,
Delighted wherever they go.

Don't stray from your course,
I direct each horse;
For the Lord says, "I am the Way."

"I'm the Truth and the Light
And everything right;
Oh, come and follow My Way!"

Lully-lu-lye, lully-lu-lye,
Hush, my baby, there's no need to cry.

Lully-lu-lye, lully-lu-lye,
Dear Jesus is always nearby.

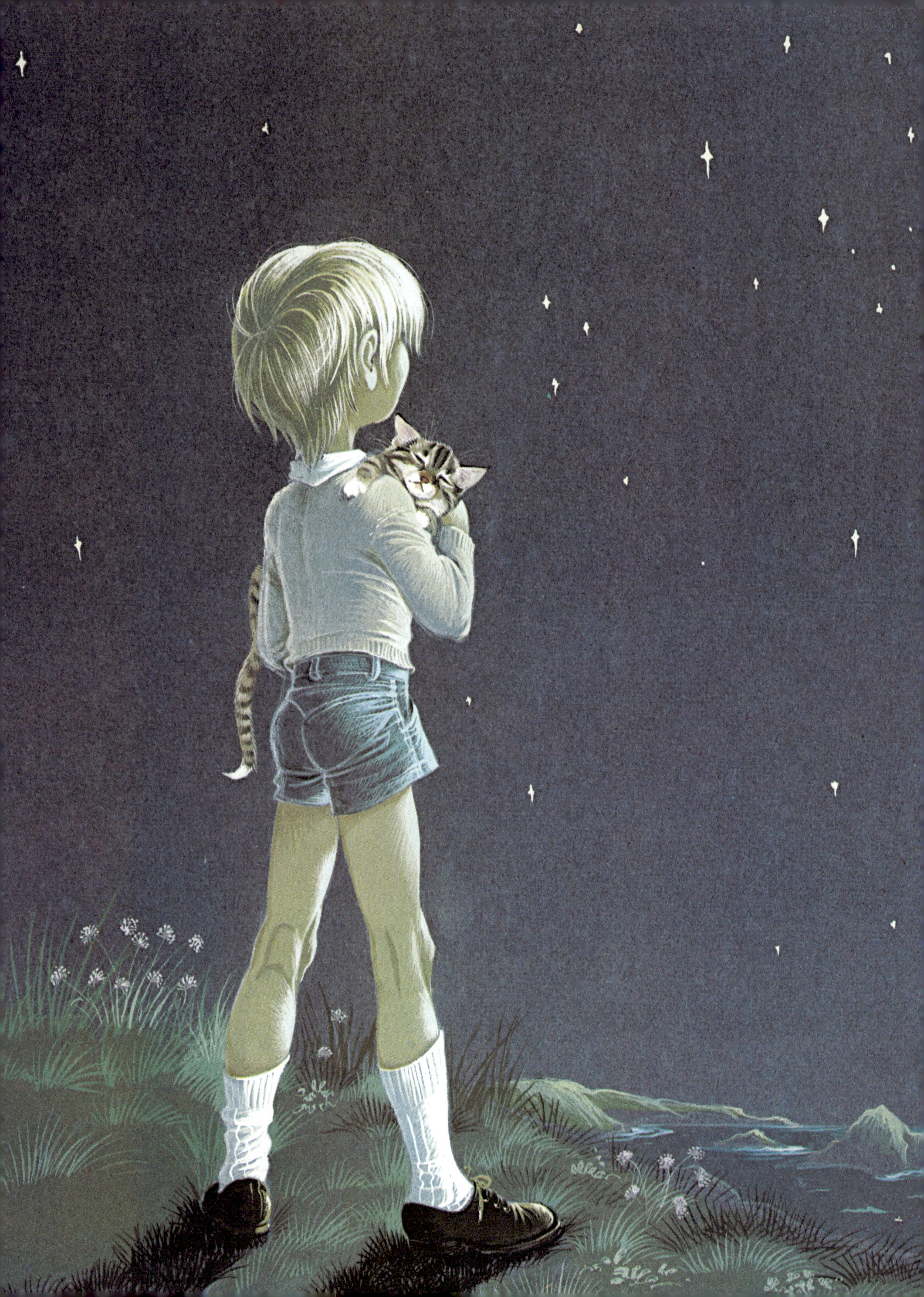

I see the moon,
And the moon sees me;
God bless the moon,
And God bless me.

Bell horses, bell horses,
What time of day?
One o'clock, two o'clock,
Time to away.

Bell horses, bell horses,
At close of day,
'Tis time for children
To bow heads and pray.

I hear skirts rustle quietly
When Mother comes to check on me;
It makes me feel so warm and safe
To know a last look she will take.

The rustling silk will follow her
When she goes out the door, quite sure
That through the night, when she's asleep,
The Lord my soul will guard and keep.